IN PRAISE OF
SOLE TRADER OR LIMITED

I0048986

Often 'how-to' guides relating to accounting and tax issues are written by the expert for other experts. This makes them incomprehensible and above the level of their target market, in this case small business owners. Anna's guide is a welcome exception to this sad rule. Her guide is clear and concise, and is pitched at exactly the right level that any small business owner can understand, and have that all-important discussion with their accountant — to incorporate or not to incorporate. Well done!

Stuart Walton, Conspicuous CBM Ltd

As a practising chartered accountant I am often asked about what structure someone should choose for their business. It's always an interesting conversation. And it's a very common question too! I'm pleased Anna has written a simple yet effective guide to help business owners better understand the benefits of a limited company. I know I'll definitely be sharing this guide with my clients and contacts. I suggest you should do the same too!

Shaz Nawaz, AA Chartered Accountants

Anna explains and guides you through a very complicated subject of sole trader vs limited company by using simple language and examples that are easily understood. As a sole trader myself, reading this book has certainly provided me with a better understanding and I now feel equipped to make that decision when it arises in the future.

Karen Pearson, Pearson Change Management

In this book, Anna writes a tour de force in simplicity. The step by step process covers all the ground needed in easy-to-understand stages. Prompted by the dialogue and supplemented by the additional questions and Appendices, an interested party can work their way through the necessary decisions, in their own time and at their own pace. What is also very helpful is the advice to work with Companies House closely, as this will both ease the process and save initial start-up costs. In the past I've set up several small companies and I've always tended to use an online service. Typical costs varied between £85 and £100, so a mere £15 via Companies House is an absolute bargain!

This is another great addition to Anna's book series and one which I recommend everyone on the cusp of this decision to buy … immediately!

John Thurlbeck, John Thurlbeck Consulting

SOLE TRADER OR LIMITED COMPANY?

ANNA GOODWIN

Sole Trader or Limited company?
Which to choose, why and the benefits and pitfalls of both

Copyright © 2015 Anna Goodwin

www.annagoodwinaccountancy.co.uk

The moral rights of Anna Goodwin to be identified as the author of this work have been asserted in accordance with the Copyright, Designs and Patents Act 1988.

Copyeditor and Proofreader: Siân-Elin Flint-Freel

Design and typesetting: Tanya Bäck (www.tanyabackdesigns.com)

Illustrator: Shirley Harvey (www.barelyrecognisable.com)

First published in 2015 by Anna Goodwin
This edition published by Anna Goodwin in 2022

ISBN 978-0-9930166-5-3

SOLE TRADER OR LIMITED COMPANY?

WHICH TO CHOOSE, WHY AND THE BENEFITS AND PITFALLS OF BOTH

ANNA GOODWIN

Hi Bert, I've been a sole trader now for 5 years and people keep suggesting I go Limited. Do you know what they're talking about?
Hi Alan, A few years ago I was considering this myself so I booked an appointment with my accountant to find out more.
The accountant explained it really well by going through the similarities and differences of a sole trader and a director and why you would do it.
I'll tell you if you like?
Yes, go for it, Bert!

WHAT IS A SOLE TRADER?

You know this, Alan, don't you because you are one now?

Alan is a sole trader

- He is an individual person – trading as 'Alan Fix It Construction Services'
- If there is a problem with his business and he can't pay the people he owes then he could lose everything, including his house – he has full liability

I know, Bert. This has always worried me and the Missus!

- He works for himself
- He can employ people, such as Shirley, his apprentice.
- He can be VAT registered

tip!

The amount of turnover you need to become VAT registered increases each year – it's £85,000 for the 22/23 tax year.

I know you're not as your turnover isn't up to the limit yet.

It's not there yet, Bert, but I'll need to keep an eye on it as it's getting close.

Well it's not difficult, Alan. When you're about to reach that level you'll need to get in touch with HMRC.

tip!

You can go VAT registered voluntarily before you reach the turnover limit. This may be beneficial if you incur a lot of expenditure that is vatable as you can reclaim it. But if your sales are primarily to individuals, not companies, it would not be a good idea as you are basically increasing the price you charge them by 20% as they can't reclaim VAT. It will also give you extra paperwork and you will need to submit your VAT returns monthly or quarterly.

Don't forget you have to submit a tax return each year, on or before 31 January, and pay any tax due by this date.

WHAT IS A LIMITED COMPANY?

> tip! It is not you trading as an individual. It's the company trading as a separate legal entity.

> You've lost me now, Bert. What's a separate legal entity? It means nothing to me.

> Don't worry! All it means is that the company is separate from you personally; any money you make isn't yours, it's the company's.

> Thanks Bert. Got it now!

As a Director of 'Alan Fix It Construction Services Limited':

- Alan would be employed by the company
- Alan's liability would be limited to the amount of share capital he introduced into the business — it is the company that is liable if his business fails

Hang on a minute, Bert. What's this about share capital?

No worries, Alan. It means if you decided to set up with £100 that's what you would be liable for.

So you can see, can't you, Alan, that this will make you and your Missus a lot less worried – you will only ever lose £1 to £1,000?

Now that sounds good, Bert. Always best to keep the Missus happy!

As a Director:

- Alan would have to submit annual accounts
- He would have to submit an annual corporation tax return (CT600)
- He would have to submit a P11D Expenses and Benefits form

In the first year of trading you may end up submitting two CT600s as the period of a CT600 can't be longer than 12 months.

Example: With an incorporation date of 6/10/22 and a year end of 31 October –
your period of accounts will be from 6/10/22 to 31/10/23 – longer than 12 months.

To summarise — this is the list my accountant gave me to show all the deadlines you will have as a director.

tip! A director of a limited company will have several filing dates which occur in the year.

Detail	Deadline
Annual accounts	9 months after the year end
Corporation tax return	12 months after the year end
Payment of corporation tax	9 months and one day after the year end
Annual return	Made up date is the anniversary of incorporation and due date is 28 days after made up date
P11Ds	6 July

But, Alan, you'll be glad to know there are a lot of similarities between being a sole trader and being a director of a limited company.

Similarities

1. Filing and recording – you still need to record your income and expenditure (see Appendix 1 for tips).
2. It's best to have a separate bank account for the business so that all business and personal items are kept separately.
3. It's best to prepare and keep to an annual budget (see appendix 2 for template).
4. You have to keep records for payroll and submit the payroll each week or month under Real Time Information (RTI) (see what this is all about in Appendix 3).

Lots to take in, Alan. Bet your head's hurting by now!

Just a bit, Bert. Thanks for explaining things to me. I'll probably need to ask you some questions as we go along.

That's fine, Alan. So, because there are lots of differences and potential pitfalls, why would you do it?

Why would you go Limited?

1. To get limited liability for your business so you are secure in the knowledge that you can't lose your house.

2. Some people do it to make their business look bigger than it is; if you're a limited company, at first glance, people won't know that you're a one-man band!

3. For some tendering of work you will need to be limited; say if you want to work for town councils.

4. In order to receive some grants you will need to be limited and VAT registered.

5. To be able to pay yourself dividends (more about that later!)

6. Psychologically it can make you feel that you have a business rather than just a hobby; it seems like the next step towards developing your business.

SETTING UP A LIMITED COMPANY

1. Go to the Companies House website –
   https://www.gov.uk/limited-company-formation

tip! Don't go to other websites as they may cost more.

2. Check under https://find-and-update.company-information.
   service.gov.uk/company-name-availability
   that the company name is available (e.g. Alan Fix It
   Construction Services Limited). If not, back to the
   drawing board.

3. If this name is available then you're ready to start
   setting your company up.

tip! Before you start setting it up you'll need to have
some information available, such as company name,
registered office address etc.
– see Bert's list in Appendix 4.

You'll be glad to know it won't take you long to go through the form and enter all of the information.

tip! If you send off all of your information to Companies House before 3pm you're likely to get the company set up by the next day — officially it takes 24 hours and costs £12.

https://www.gov.uk/limited-company-formation/register-your-company

tip! Once you've completed and submitted the form, you'll receive a Certificate of Incorporation and Memorandum and Articles of Association.

Your Certificate of Incorporation will be dated. This will give you the first day of your accounting period — not necessarily your first day of trading!

Once you receive your Certificate of Incorporation you can set up your business bank account.

To set up a business bank account you will need the originals of:

- Certificate of Incorporation
- Passport/Driving licence
- Utility bill

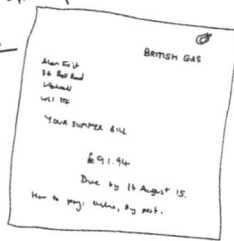

Once you have your business bank account set up, you can start!

tip! If you have transferred from being a sole trader to a director of a limited company there will be a period when you will be paying for things personally and receiving income personally. It's best to keep a list of this income and expenditure.

When I was thinking of trading as a limited company, Alan, the accountant said that there are some areas that might trip me up so I think it's best to look at these straight away.

BANK ACCOUNT
ALAN FIX IT CONTROL LTD

Sounds like a plan!

tip!

Director's Current Account

Do not take out or deposit any money into the business bank account that relates to you personally.

I said to the accountant, "What do I do then?" Sounded impossible to me. An expense sheet is the answer!

tip!

Enter any personal expenditure that you make on behalf of the company on an expense sheet (see Appendix 5) and then withdraw the total amount out of the bank account monthly.

Expense Tracking

DATE DESCRIPTION   £   TAX   NI   %   TOTAL

TOTAL

But why is it so important, Bert? I've managed to trade all these years without having a business account and always having a mixture of business and private items.

It's because it's not your company, Alan. You are just an employee. Any personal items will be posted to a Director's Current Account.*

*see Appendix 6 for more information

PAYING YOURSELF AS A DIRECTOR OF A LIMITED COMPANY

Alan, this will all be completely new to you, it was to me, so I'll go through it and then if you're stuck let me know.

OK Bert, sounds good.

Well, as a sole trader, if you need any money you can take it out of the business profits as they are all yours. It is good to have a set amount that you take out each week or month but it is possible to take cash out as you need it.

As a director of a limited company, this is completely different and you will usually be paid a mixture of salary and dividends.

A dividend is a sum of money paid regularly (either monthly, quarterly or annually) by a company out of its profits.

In order to pay out a dividend, a meeting is held by all the directors agreeing the amount to be paid to each director and the date of the payment. A dividend voucher is completed and signed by all the directors.

tip!

Usually, directors are paid monthly up to the National Insurance limit of £12,570 in 22/23 or up to the personal allowance limit of £12,570. Dividends will then be added to the salary to give a total amount withdrawn from the business.

Date _/_/_

EXPENSES
UK Pay

Gross Pay
TOTAL
Deductions/
TAX
REFUND
NET PAY

Example:

| Salary | £11,908 | Paid £992.33 per month |
| Dividend | £20,000 | Paid £5,000 per quarter |

It is important that you recognise that the salary and dividends taken out of the business will affect your personal tax and corporation tax differently.

PERSONAL TAX WITHIN YOUR SELF-ASSESSMENT RETURN

There is no tax or National Insurance employees to pay on the salary and no tax to pay on the dividends as they are below the basic rate band of £37,700 in 22/23.

CORPORATE TAX IN THE COMPANY ACCOUNTS

The salary is an allowable deduction to reduce the amount of profits of the company and hence the amount of corporation tax is paid at 19%. The dividend is not taken into account when calculating the profits for corporation tax.

tip:
A word of warning. Dividends cannot be paid out by a company if there are not sufficient profits in the business to cover the dividends.

Thanks very much for explaining all of this to me, Bert. It's been incredibly useful! But I have a final question.

OK, go for it!

It seems like there is a lot to think about and possibilities for getting things wrong! Do you think having an accountant would be a good idea?

I think for anyone who is a director of a limited company an accountant is essential.

As a director, having an accountant:

- Saves you time
- Gives you peace of mind
- Ensures everything is done properly; only tax deductible expenditure claimed
- Gives you confidence that all HMRC paperwork is being dealt with as it all goes to your accountant as well as you
- All accounts, corporation tax returns, annual returns etc. are submitted online
- Is someone there to provide ongoing business advice and guidance
- Means they set everything up for you so that you are using the correct templates for expenses sheets, dividend vouchers etc.

So there we are, Alan, that's everything. The benefits are that you have security, it can give the initial impression that your business is bigger than it is and you can pay yourself dividends. Conversely, you will have increased accountancy costs and more paperwork and recording.

Overall I think it's a good idea, Bert, and I'm going to go for it!

BOOKKEEPING 2022/23

But will it affect me?

No, not at all. You will receive your salary as you normally do.

I didn't realise it was so easy to become a company director of a Limited company. Thanks Bert!

ALAN FIX-IT CONSTRUCTION SERVICES LTD.

APPENDIX 1: TIPS FOR FILING/RECORDING

FILE
TIP

IMPORTANT

Choose the system that
suits _you_.

INCOME - Filing

- Keep all income receipts
- File numerically – start at 1
- File in date order – start at 1st April if your
  year end is 31st March

INCOME - Recording

- Manually — In a bookkeeping book – list
  each receipt throughout the
  month and total at the end
  of the month.

- Computerised — As above but on the
  spreadsheet — computer.

- Accounting — As above but on the
  software package — computer.

BOOKKEEPING
2022/23

EXPENSES - Filing

- Keep all receipts — If you're not sure they are
  tax deductible, then ask.

- File numerically — Number them yourself,
  starting at 1, rather than
  using the invoice number
  automatically entered – this
  is usually massive and you'll
  waste time writing it out.

- File in date — Start at 1st April if your
  order — year end is 31st March.

EXPENSES - Recording

- Manually
OR - Computerised spreadsheet
OR - Accounting software package

Make a list of each entry, analysed into the relevant expenditure:

- Purchases
- Motor expenses
- Travel including accommodation
- Wages
- Rent, rates, insurance

- Repairs
- Accountancy
- Bank interest / charges
- Telephone
- Stationery

etc. – and total at the end of the month

APPENDIX 2: ANNUAL BUDGET TEMPLATE

Business Name:
12 Month Period from:

Budget	November £	December £	January £	February £	
Income					
Direct Costs					
Gross Profit	0.00	0.00	0.00	0.00	
Gross Profit %					
Travel					
Accomodation					
Resources					
Subsistence					
Telephone -					
Mobile					
Subscriptions					
Insurance					
Memberships					
Training					
Marketing					
Printing					
Postage &					
Stationary					
Total	0.00	0.00	0.00	0.00	
Net Profit	0.00	0.00	0.00	0.00	
Net Profit %					
Year to date					

APPENDIX 3: REAL TIME INFORMATION (RTI)

All employers must report PAYE in real time. Each time you pay an employee you must submit details about employee's pay and deductions to HMRC using payroll software.

APPENDIX 4: INFORMATION REQUIRED TO INCORPORATE A COMPANY

- Proposed name
- Each Director(s) names and addresses – both residential and business
- Each Director(s) occupation(s)
- Each Director(s) date of birth
- Security information for each Director – last 3 digits of phone number, colour of eyes, place of birth
- Registered office address
- Name and address of Company Secretary
- Total issued share capital – this is normally in round amounts – say £1, £10, £100 or £1,000

A **Certificate of Incorporation** is a legal document relating to the formation of a company or corporation. It is a license to form a corporation issued by state government.

The **Memorandum of Association** is the document that sets up the company and the **Articles of Association** set out how the company is run, governed and owned.

INCORPORATION OF COMPANY — COSTS AND POSTAL SERVICE INFORMATION

Online applications are usually registered within 24 hours and cost £12 (paid by debit or credit card or Paypal).

Postal applications take 8 to 10 days and cost £40 (paid by cheque made out to 'Companies House').

There's a same day service costing £100. You must get your application to Companies House by 3pm. Your envelope (and any courier's envelope) must be marked 'same day service' in the top left-hand corner.

APPENDIX 5: DETAILED SUMMARY OF EXPENSES TEMPLATE

Name:
Date Paid:

Travel expenses (T)
Networking (N)
Mileage (M)
Salary (S)
Stamps, Stationery etc (PPS)
Home costs (H)
Telephone (TE)
Other costs (O)

Current slip no.	Date	Code	Description	Amount
1				
2				
3				
4				
5				
6				
7				
8				
9				
10				
11				
			Total	0.00

Travel expenses (train, taxi, parking,...)			
Mileage @ 45p per mile			
Subsistence			
Networking			
Stamps, Stationery			
Other			
Home costs			
Telephone			
Total			0.00

APPENDIX 6: DIRECTOR'S CURRENT ACCOUNT

Also known as DLA, Director's Current Account or DCA - this is a record of all transactions between a director and the company. Typically transactions may include monies loaned to the company by the director and expense claims where he/she has used personal monies to pay for company costs.

ACCOUNTING GUIDES

I have always worked closely with my clients and aim to empower them so that they know more about their accounts and can do more themselves. With this in mind, I have devised a series of Simple Accountancy Guides so that business owners can do some of the figure work themselves.

- *Anna's Simple Accounting Guides – Stress Free Tax Returns*
  Be better prepared for HMRC and know what to give your accountant and when.
  Simple and easy to understand
- *Anna's Simple Accountancy Guides – Quick and Easy Guide to Bank Reconcilliations*

Also available:

- *Your Business, Your Numbers*
  Improve your business growth and have the confidence to tackle profit and loss, balance sheets and much more.
- *Accountants Don't Bite – Improve Your Relationship With Your Accountant To Maximise Growth And Profitability*
  How to develop an excellent relationship with your accountant and how you can work together to improve your business.

Please keep up to date with the guides and what Alan and Bert are up to by liking my Facebook author page.

www.facebook.com/AnnatheauthorGoodwin

www.ingramcontent.com/pod-product-compliance
Lightning Source LLC
Chambersburg PA
CBHW040911210326
41597CB00029B/5049